A HERO
LIKE NO OTHER

KATIE DAVIDSON

CONTRIBUTORS

··

Illustrator:
KATIE GRACE
HERSHBERGER

Editors:
AUDREY DIAL
JENNIE HEIDEMAN
HELEN HUMMEL
ALLI MCDOUGAL

Some heroes fly high, gliding bravely through the breeze.
Others lift heavy objects like cars and trucks with ease.

Some heroes run fast, zooming by with lightning speed,

but I know the greatest Hero—
the Hero who sets me free.

This hero's name is Jesus.

He is strong, and He is kind.

He heals the sick, raises the dead,
and gives hope to all mankind!

By just the sound of His voice,
He calms the winds and rain.

And He feeds five thousand men
with just two loaves of grain!

But these big miracles are just
the beginning of His story...

for Jesus, our greatest Hero, is full
of wonder and power and glory.

To understand our Hero, we must understand His foe:
His enemy named Satan, who wants bad things to grow.

Satan's sneaky plan
convinced God's people to sin.

And his evil plan worked—
God's people disobeyed Him.

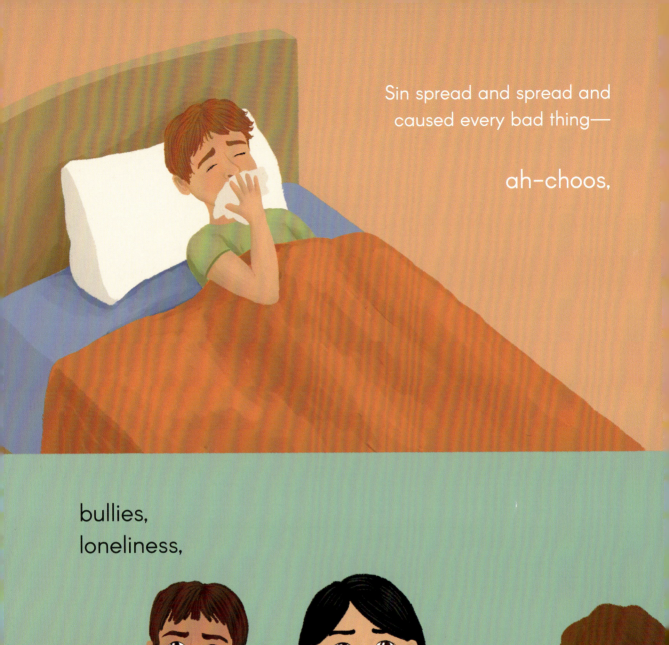

Sin spread and spread and caused every bad thing—

ah-choos,

bullies,
loneliness,

and even bee stings!

This problem called sin lives
in my heart and yours too.

It's when we talk back, yell,
or say something untrue!

God hates sin, for He is good
and sin is not.

So in His love, He decided to ruin
Satan's sneaky plot.

God sent Jesus, the greatest Hero,
to save us from our sin

so that God and His people
would be together again.

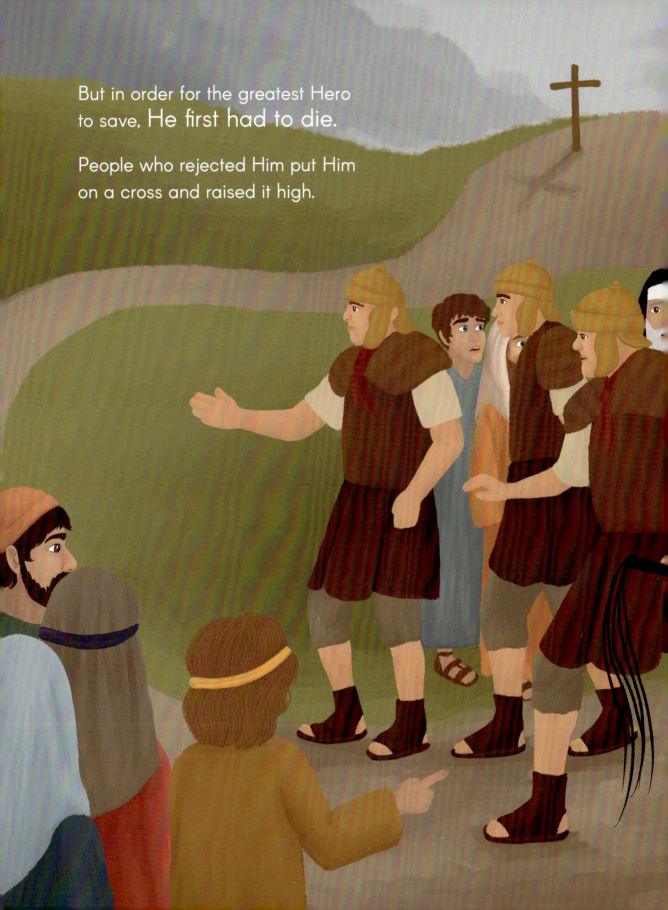

But in order for the greatest Hero
to save, He first had to die.

People who rejected Him put Him
on a cross and raised it high.

No, Jesus did not have a super suit
or wear a fancy cape.

Instead, Jesus wore humility.
He did not try to escape.

Yes, the greatest Hero felt all the
pain of our sins that day.

It was the saddest day there ever was.
Darkness filled the skies.

God's people thought all hope was lost.
Our greatest Hero died.

But this is not the end of the story.

Do not worry, do not fret!

Satan thought He had won,
but Jesus wasn't finished yet.

Jesus's body was placed in a tomb
for three days.

Then on the third, our greatest Hero
was not found in the grave!

It was the best day there ever was.
Jesus rose in victory!

And just like that, our greatest Hero
crushed His enemy!

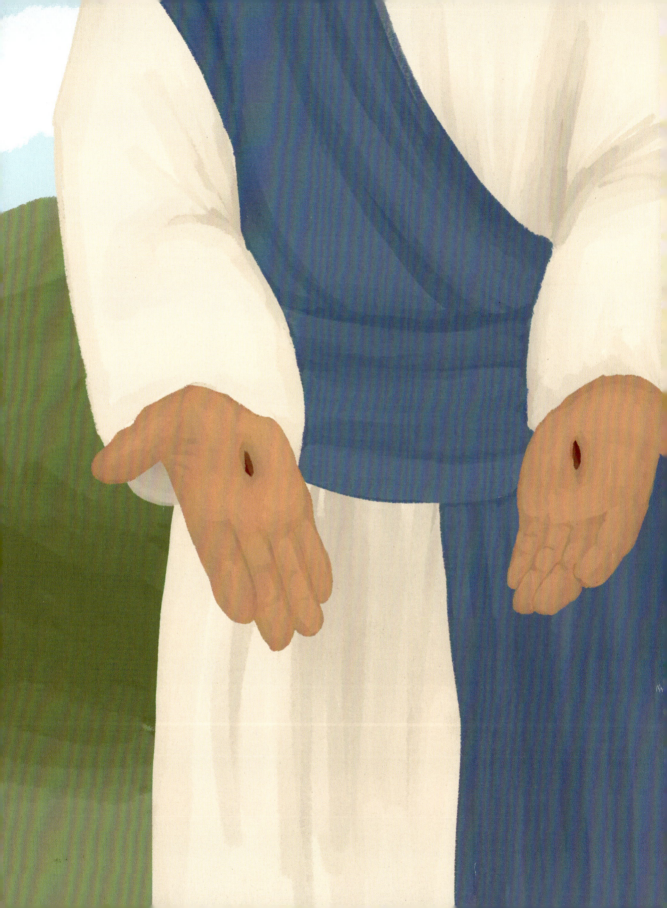

Jesus did not lift heavy objects
or zoom by with lightning speed,

but He saved God's people from
sin. His death has set us free!

What good news!
What great joy!
We are thankful for today.

There is no battle too big for Jesus,
so we don't have to be afraid.

Yes, no matter what tomorrow holds,
we can confidently say,

"Jesus Christ is our greatest Hero,
forever and always."

Thank You for studying God's Word with us!

CONNECT WITH US

@thedailygraceco @dailygracepodcast

CONTACT US

info@thedailygraceco.com

SHARE

#thedailygraceco

VISIT US ONLINE

www.thedailygraceco.com